MEDITATION & SPIRITUALITY
A PHILOSOPHY

BY

SHIV MATHUR

A PATH TO ATTAIN A STEADY MEDITATIVE STATE

<u>PREFACE</u>

I was born in Varanasi on 09th March 1966. It was an auspicious day as on that day it was a major Indian festival called "Mahashivaratri". I completed my schooling in Kota, Rajasthan and then did Electrical Engineering from REC Warangal, Andhra Pradesh, India in the year 1989. Thereafter, I joined the Indian Navy. I got married in October 1991 and we were blessed with a daughter in November 1994. Life was hectic while working in the Indian Navy but at the same time it had taught me discipline, idealism, humanity and leadership. By the time I reached the age of 50, our daughter had completed her college education in France. She then started working from the year 2017.

We all go through various challenges in life, and so did I. This made me question about the reality of life and what are we made to chase. What are we finally getting from this chase? So this chase and struggle in the materialistic world where one is trying to meet all the worldly aspirations and commitments, led to a sub conscious awakening and questioning. Finally in 2015, when I was about to be free from all my family & worldly commitments, I got drawn towards the Himalayas, or rather Rishikesh to be more precise.

My regular visits to Rishikesh, and subsequently to other places across the Dev Bhoomi (Land of Gods) started happening. Almost twice every year, I was there, spending two weeks on each visit. Later, spending even longer periods of time. All my visits were full of explorations in the areas nearby, trying to find some real saints and yogis. Simultaneously, I had also got drawn towards devotional music or bhajans/kirtans. I was listening to them for hours every day before going to sleep and even while driving to the office in the car. I also started watching videos of teachings of some of the prominent saints & yogis of yesteryear. Like, Yogananda, Ramana Maharishi, Swami Rama, Swami Vivekananda, Nisargdutta Guru Maharaj, Neemkaroli Baba, Shri Yukteshwar Giri ji.

Circumstances made me quit my job in Mar 2019. It was also a desire, or rather an intention, to quit working by 2019 and pursue spirituality as my passion and profession.

During my visits to the Himalayas, I came across a few real yogis and also found some places where some realized yogis had lived before. The first experience itself transformed me completely. This was in 2015 at Tatwale Baba's cave near Rishikesh. Perhaps I was prepared to receive his grace, so it got bestowed upon me. This happened during my first visit to his cave. It seems that I was subconsciously preparing myself for my spiritual path, so when one is making an effort, then grace also gets gifted. The experience was of my mind going thoughtless, and since then it has stayed like that. Thoughtless means, that, if I am working on something, then only thoughts related to that will come. If I am not doing anything, then I can remain practically thoughtless.

I had a few more out of time and space experiences at Acharya Bhaskar Joshi ji's place in Devprayag.

As the mind got de-cluttered, I started getting answers and understood that how did all this happen. What got revealed was the whole process and method, which I went through sub-consciously, and which finally lead me to this stable mental state.

I realized that if this can also be achieved by others who are seeking in the spiritual realm, then this could be a great service which I can render to them. While staying in the ashrams in Rishikesh, I had noticed that many people, especially westerners, were travelling to India to seek the spiritual wisdom and learn yoga. What I observed was that they were unable to get that true wisdom and what was offered in these ashrams, was a tailor made package of yoga asana and some meditation techniques. There are many young yoga teachers teaching in these ashrams and they do not seem to have any experiential knowledge. These ashrams have slowly become more and more commercialized. Though overall, it is definitely a different and good experience. For many seekers, these ashrams are like a gateway to the spiritual path. Maybe these are good for beginners or just casual visitors. Though the Gurus who opened these ashrams were realized souls. Shivananda ashram in Rishikesh was started by the self realized yogi Swami Shivananda. Many seekers benefited from his presence and his discourses.

Therefore, I thought if I can transmit whatever I have gained through my spiritual journey then I would feel that my life has been a fulfilling experience. It is important to give back to society. Therefore, I started teaching in Europe from July 2018 onwards during my visits and later when I moved to Poland in March 2019. It was like taking the teachings to the doorstep of the seekers from Europe. Due to the onset of Corona pandemic in March 2020, my classes came to a halt. During the lockdown in Warsaw, I decided to upload some videos on You Tube of my Himalayan travels and my meetings with some real yogis. A few of those videos received a good response. I then went on to make some more videos on the subject of meditation and spirituality. In November 2020, I had to return to India. I was asked by some friends, that, why don't I write a book. Finally the time came in May 2022, and here I am penning down my thoughts about this whole process. Everything happens when the time comes and if it has to happen.

I am thankful to God and all the saints and yogis whose guidance and grace, is guiding me in this journey of life. I also thank my parents for what they did in bringing me up and making me into a human worthy of living. I hope this book helps seekers in getting some clarity. If the philosophy is found useful, then it would be great, as it can help transform a seeker.

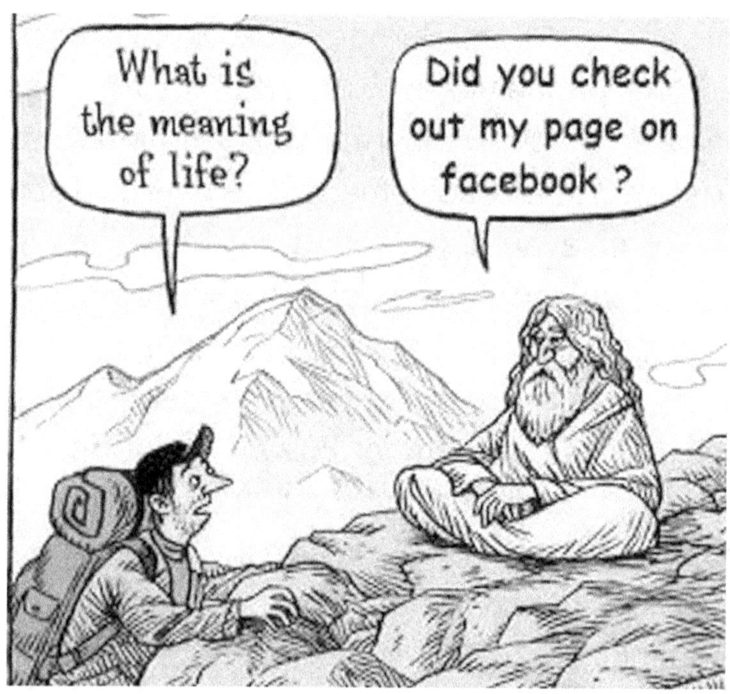

TABLE OF CONTENTS

CHAPTER - 1

INTRODUCTION TO MEDITATION

1.1 WHAT IS MEDITATION – LET US DEFINE IT

1.11 Meditation can be defined in many ways. The prime goal of meditation for most people should be to achieve a steady state of peace, content and calm. In other words, achieving a state of eternal happiness, or internal happiness. I would say that this can be the first goal for all. In my understanding, there could be various stages or milestones in the goal of meditation.

1.12 Another way of describing the goal of meditation is to achieve self-realization, finding true self, realization of absolute truth, reality of life, finding oneself, finding God, connecting with God, raising the conscious level to a higher consciousness or higher plane, removing negative thoughts, living in the present and not in the past or future, controlled mind, stable mind, taming the mind, purification of mind, enlightenment, understanding creation, attainment of ultimate knowledge of creation, de-stressing oneself, getting rid of worries, etc.

1.13 Meditation might have been initiated by the ancient Indian Sages. One thing which is very interesting to note is that the word in Sanskrit or Hindi for meditation is DHYAN. Dhyan means focus or attention. Only after attaining a focused mind, one can achieve success in the final goals of meditation. Therefore, the mind has to be trained, or I would say reprogrammed, to reach a meditative state.

1.14 Once this goal is achieved in meditation, then one can go beyond to the higher realms of consciousness, thereby attaining the knowledge of creation. In other words, by staying at a higher awareness level or at a higher consciousness level, one can then seek the knowledge and get the experiences which are beyond space and time. This can be the next goal.

1.15 So meditation can be described in many ways, but it means all the same. What is required is, that we understand the different stages, and the process to reach the various stages.

1.16 **Therefore, what we want to achieve in meditation needs to be clear**. We will focus only on the first goal, which is "Attaining a steady state of calm and contentment". This is so because, as I write this book, it is based on my personal explorations, discoveries, and experiences. I can only explain what I have experienced. When we read from other sources and become knowledgeable through the books, it is very different from learning through direct experience. Reading, listening can be a guide, but without direct experience, it may not be fulfilling and in-depth.

1.2 <u>BOOKS WHERE MEDITATION IS DESCRIBED AS IN THE ANCIENT INDIAN SCRIPTURES</u>

1.2.1 There are various books which define what meditation is and how to meditate. The **Yog Sutras** is the most referred one in most yoga schools and teacher training courses. This was written by **Sage Patanjali,** who codified the entire process in a logical sequence. Sutra means stitching up the entire puzzle or connecting all the pieces. That is why this philosophy is so interlinked, so much so, that one needs to keep flowing and interconnecting with every aspect. Other books are Vedas, Upanishads & Bhagavad Gita, and I guess, a few more, written later by many self realized saints, for the benefit of the humanity. Sage Patanjali had given a methodical approach to the in-depth meaning of yog. It explains the method for achieving the various stages. He had given eight steps in which meditation is the seventh stage, the final being Samadhi. Yog (Yoga, a is silent in Yoga, but people pronounce it incorrectly) is not just asanas but it is the union of mind with self where one merges with consciousness. Yog is generally seen as mere asana practice or a fitness regime. In reality, asanas are just one of the initial steps of Yog. The initial stages are related to control of the body through asanas (postures), food intake, and the withdrawal of sense, which enables you to go inwards. Pranayam is breathing control. Asanas are very important aspects, as in order to meditate, one has to master one asana (posture). It is during this asan that one will have to stay still while meditating. If a person cannot stay still in a posture, like a sitting posture on the floor with the spine straight, then it will not be possible to have a still mind. As for the body that cannot stay still, that body will keep bothering the person's mind. This is a very important condition and people should keep this in mind, especially, when you go to a meditation teacher expecting that the teacher will do some magic and you will be able to meditate. Without practicing the asana one cannot move forward with control of mind. Patanjali Yog Sutra has explained meditation as a step wise process.

Unfortunately, every seeker or learner is looking at this concept as a mechanical means or a physical technique, whereas this has a deep philosophical meaning. For example withdrawal of senses, this is a very deep subject and this is what I am going to explain in this book. As this is a topic of discussion here and this is nothing but the dharma and karma theory of Vedanta. I would say this is nothing but understanding and following humanity. This sounds weird but this is what it is.

1.2.2 Another good book specifically on meditation is "The Complete Book of Yoga" by Swami Vivekananda.

1.2.3 Then we have "**Conquest of Mind**" by Swami Shivananda. I would personally recommend this book to all the seekers.

1.2.4 The MOST IMPORTANT MESSAGE ALL THESE BOOKS GIVE IS THAT LEARN THROUGH DIRECT EXPERIENCE and don't get stuck to book learning. Despite the key message, everyone is scurrying for knowledge in books, and don't use that as a clue to go beyond the book learning. Jnana Yog is one of the four paths to self-realization and that is followed by using one's own intellect to seek the knowledge through experiences one gets in life.

1.3 <u>WHEN DO WE REALISE THAT WE REALLY NEED TO MEDITATE</u>

1.3.1 The problem is that the modern education system does not teach us anything about humanity or human development. The modern system and the lifestyle have completely misguided us as far as personal/human development is considered. As a result, we have been churning out generations after generations whose foundation as a human beings is very weak. Students graduating out of college are clueless about life and the real goals of life. As we start running after the material acquisitions for which we have been trained and we start distancing ourselves from nature, we end up on the wrong runway with no escape. A society whose foundation is money, capitalism, consumerism, and materialism, is producing humans whose main traits are greed, selfishness, ego, ignorance, lust, hatred, jealousy, and so on. Life becomes stressful by the day and no one knows what is happening to them until the body and mind are so abused that we enter a phase of health issues – mental as well as physical. For health issues depending on their seriousness, we take recourse to modern medicine, which is a quick and temporary fix. We continue to run on the same highway or runway till we reach a burn out or more severe health as well as mental issues. Some spend their whole life like this and don't want to know what is happening. The tendency is to blame others for all your worldly miseries. I meet old people who are so stressed but are unable to find what is going wrong. Some or few want to figure out what is going wrong, provided their ego is melted a bit. Ego is the biggest barrier in most for not allowing us to look inwards and find out what is going wrong. Only on being kicked consistently by life's experiences, do some of us start questioning and some of us start finding out what needs to be done. That is when we come to know of these ancient practices of meditation and spiritual theories, found by the ancient wise humans, saints, yogis, and philosophers. Then starts the search for wise men/women who can guide us, heal us, and help transform us. Effectively, society has lost the primary reference of humanity and is so lost that it does not know where to find it. Religious books if studied properly are a great guide towards humanity, be it Bhagavad Gita or Upanishads or Bible, etc. One needs to study these books oneself and not run for courses and discourses. Hard work and self-effort is needed to find the foundation of the existence and operations of human beings.

1.3.2 Thousands of years ago the sages and yogis in India found these techniques said to be conveyed none other than by Lord Shiva known as Adiyogi. He conveyed this yogic science to seven Rishis. The constellation in the sky known as Ursa Major is known in India as the seven sisters or SaptRishis. Sapt means seven and Rishis means Sages. These seven sages were given seven sciences.

1.3.3 Therefore, those who want to meditate are the ones who have finally realized that it is time to get out of the illusionary materialistic trap and find out the reality and finally achieve peace of mind. Some want to get peace of mind but do not want to leave the materialistic lifestyle, but the fact is that they have at least realized that peace of mind is needed.

1.3.4 Therefore, this philosophy helps in gradually getting you to understand how to live in this materialistic world but at the same time have peace of mind. The formula is that one can live happily in this materialistic world provided one is completely detached from this materialistic world. The focus is on performing one's duties/**Karma** as per the **Dharma**.

1.3.5 We will go deep into this whole philosophy. My aim is that through this book you may get the key to open the door yourself and tread this path of self-realization and happiness. The key is to use your intellect and questioning ability, analyzing ability, and logical reasoning to find out, what is there in this journey of life. All the answers are inscribed inside our souls. We have to only start exploring and start asking the right questions to ourselves, truthfully and sincerely.

1.3.6 The aim is to stop believing what everyone is saying, stop following what is the general perception, and go for finding the truth yourself. Believe in someone whom you have the confidence that the person knows and not what is in the air. Otherwise, we will fall in the category of gossip followers. Our ability to correctly use our discriminatory abilities to make the right judgment about everything is what is needed. We have to learn how to develop our discriminatory abilities. Here I quote a saying of Swami Rama, that all that you have read in the books is not your own findings but someone else's findings. Someone else found through their own experience and intellect and reasoning. Therefore, this book is not being written to make you knowledgeable through my experiences, but to trigger your curiosity and drive you to go out and search for yourself. This is just a guide. Self-realization is like a treasure hunt where you will get clues, but finally, you have to go hunting yourself. Remember the "Snakes & Ladders" board game.

THE PHILOSOPHY

THE FOUR PILLARS

1. HOW MIND WORKS

2. HUMAN DESIGN OR HUMAN MIRROR OR <u>DHARMA</u>

3. ROLES AND RESPONSIBILITIES OR <u>KARMA</u>

4. ENERGY CORRELATION OF THOUGHTS

1.4.1 We can divide this whole philosophy into four major sections as depicted above. We saw the definitions of Meditation in the previous paragraphs, now we will move to the core philosophy which is divided into four sections. The next four chapters will take us deeper into these four pillars of this philosophy.

1.4.2 Human beings have been designed for a specific purpose. Every creation in this world has a specific purpose and it has been provided certain characteristics and features by God (creator) for enabling it to achieve its goals. There cannot be a random creation so there has to be uniformity in creation. **Dharma** is nothing but the characteristics of humans based on which the humans should carry out their tasks or duties/responsibilities. Dharma is like a rule book for optimum performance of human beings. There is no other way out for humans, if they have to tread their life on a well-defined path. Humans have the intellect and willpower which needs to be used to tread on the correct path and eventually get released from the cycle of birth and death. When a person dies it is said he/she passed away, though the body only dies what passes away is the soul. After death, people don't use the name but say take the body away. The soul is the real identity, which is immortal. The cycle of birth and death continues and the soul continues its journey from one life form to another life form, till it gets the human life and is able to get liberated from this cycle and merge in this vast consciousness or the source of its creation. This seems to be a logical conclusion and if this is not the logical conclusion what else can be the other reason for living in this world. This is a very deep topic of discussion and many at this point in time will agree or disagree with this theory. So we can maybe ignore it at this point in time, but the design of humans is very logical as nothing in this world is created randomly. One can see humans as one of the products of this creation. Our ego thinks that humans are a different kind of material and above every other creature on this planet. That is why we have distanced ourselves from co-existence with nature. By nature, I mean the entire creation. The feeling of oneness is lost, and oneness comes when one lives with raised awareness and consciousness after realizing the absolute truth of the creation and human existence.

Dharma is nothing but the correct human characteristics or human qualities, on which every human action and thought is to be based while performing all the **KARMA**s/ tasks/duties. We can also call it the constitution of humans, like the constitution of a country. It is like the LAW. I called it human design and created a human mirror where every individual can look into it to understand where they stand with respect to the correctness of their characteristics.

Once we have understood Karma and Dharma and their interlinking, then we can go to see what triggers the thoughts and how the **Mind Work**. How does every karma create a thought negative or positive (happiness or sadness) based on whether the karma was as per the dharma or not as per the dharma. I think this is clear now. We will deliberate on this topic in detail subsequently.

Lastly, we will see how is the collective energy field created continuously by the actions or karmas we execute or just the thoughts which are getting generated continuously. As thoughts are an outcome of the inputs the brain gets from the five sensory organs and the memory.

CHAPTER - 2

MIND

HOW MIND WORKS

2.   WHAT IS THE TARGET OBJECT IN MEDITATION – **MIND** ?

2.1   The target is the mind, as that is what is troubling us and that is what needs to be controlled and stabilized. If the mind is stabilized then we can reach a state where there is peace, calmness, contentment, and happiness. This is the first battle to be won and it is like the first milestone in the path of meditation. The next milestone is to realize who we are and that is like the final realization where you connect and identify yourself with your soul and merge with the consciousness, universe, or God.

2.2   If we agree that MIND is our target and the object and the subject, then don't we think that we need to understand how the mind works?

Once the working of the mind is known then one will know how to reprogram the mind and make it work as per need. Then instead of our mind controlling us, we will be able to control our mind. The mind will stop wandering or stop running untamed. Therefore, meditation is all about taming the mind and making it available whenever needed.

2.3　We also need to understand that, why is our mind controlling us and why is it behaving in a certain way. As this leads to the generation of unwanted thoughts or worries, and it gets worst with time. The mind is gradually programmed based on each and every person's upbringing. External societal influences and teachings one undergoes create patterns. This programs the mind to act and process in a certain way. Once we identify the wrong patterns, we can instruct our mind to correct them. By practicing the changed pattern repeatedly we will be able to change the earlier pattern. Hence the mind gets re-programmed to act correctly as per the perfect human design or human qualities/ characteristics. We all say that one should be a good human being but there is no effort from anyone to understand in detail that, what is being good. Therefore, there is no effort made to live like a good human being. We are a slave to worldly distractions, and that is why we are actually a slave to our mind which has been harassing us for long. This is the real reason for all the suffering, as sufferings are what is created and perceived by the mind.

2.4   We also need to understand the origin or generation of thoughts, and from where are they generated. Which are the triggers for such thoughts?

Therefore, step-wise we will see how the whole process flow happens.

The source of thought is sensory organs and thoughts (memories) stored in the memory. We have five sensory organs from which inputs are sent to the brain where the signal is processed. Like whatever we see is sensed by the eyes and the act is called "seeing" or "sighting", whatever is seen with open eyes is sent to the brain through the nerves. Nerves are carriers of the signal between the sensory organ and the brain. The signal has to be processed in the brain. As every input to the brain from any of the sensory organ is in form of an electric signal, therefore, it has energy. Based on the way the brain has been programmed, it processes the input signal and generates an output signal. The logic here is that energy gets transformed and every input has to have an output. Therefore, once the brain has received the signal it will process it according to the program it has been installed with just like an OS - Operating System inside a computer. Here to understand the functioning of a human being we can draw an analogy with the Computer. The programming of the brain is actually the upbringing of a person from childhood onwards. It also depends on the past karma of the person and the destiny of that person. The past life journey is carried forward in the next lives. This is the journey of the soul which we are transiting through, and not the journey of the body.

Apart from the five sensory organs, the brain will also receive input signals from the memory of the person. There also seem to be sub-conscious memories where perhaps the past birth memories are stored. The sub-conscious memory remains inaccessible conspicuously to the person.

What is stored in the memory are the events in one's life which have left some impact on that person. These can be sweet memories, sad memories, or traumas. These stored events or memories keep sending signals to the brain at varying intervals depending upon the impact they had on one's psyche. Sometimes it is difficult to forget a few events or happenings in one's life and such signals keep pounding on the brain at a higher frequency and intensity, consistently creating constant worries or negative thoughts, leading to a preoccupation with sadness and maybe depression.

So it becomes more important to understand this whole process of thought generation, in the mind. We have seen that the triggers of the thoughts are coming from the sensory organs and the memory. We therefore, need to understand how the brain processes them. In a way how was the brain programmed.

For example, if a person does not like a black colour cat, that indicates that right from the first time the person saw a black cat and someone told that a black cat is not good, that person will had this input to the brain that black cat is not good. So every time a black cat is seen, the person will keep telling himself, oh ! The black cat! It is not good. After sometime this will get etched in his brain that black cat is not good. So it is basically what one grows up being taught in school, amongst friends or at home, or what one reads or watches either through digital means or print or direct viewing of any event, that one starts to form opinions. The teachings or the learning, while growing from childhood onwards, start forming perceptions or patterns. These patterns can also be called habits or the understanding of each individual. So what is the problem here? It is just that, when the learning or teachings are incorrect, then the same will get engraved in the brain, and this is what we call programming of the brain. These become the characteristics or traits or nature of a person. As everything is ever-changing in this world, there is always a possibility of getting new patterns or changing of existing patterns.

Now, why is it so that everyone has a different upbringing without a standard reference? While in schools and colleges only modern education is imparted, but there are no teachings about humanity. Therefore, as far as personal development is concerned, there are no standard teachings followed anywhere in this modern society. Now, what is that standard foundation or teachings, which should be the benchmark and taught to every individual in this world. THIS IS WHAT IS CALLED DHARMA. It is a kind of law or we can also say human design. It describes the right qualities of a human being.

In order to understand thought generation, we will only discuss one quality here. As Dharma or Human Design will be discussed in detail in chapter 4.

One of the qualities we will discuss now is "Not being Jealous" or "Always happy to see others happy or prospering or progressing". If a person was got groomed in such a way that he/she tends to generally get jealous in most situations, then obviously such a person's brain will generate a negative thought or sad feeling or unhappiness. Another way around, a non-jealous quality is considered to be a standard human quality, a positive human quality. Now no one needs to tell us what is good to have quality and what is not good for humans. This is all embedded in our souls. This is also the true nature of all humans – to have all positive good human qualities or human values. We can list all the good qualities one by one. Then see how we assess each quality with respect to our own self. Then one by one we can see how each quality is making an impact in generating a type of thought in our mind.

I am sure you have understood well enough the process of thought generation in the mind. The sensory organs, the nerves sending the signal from the sensory organ to the brain, then the brain processing that signal based on its pre-programmed patterns, and finally the net output in form of positive or negative thought.

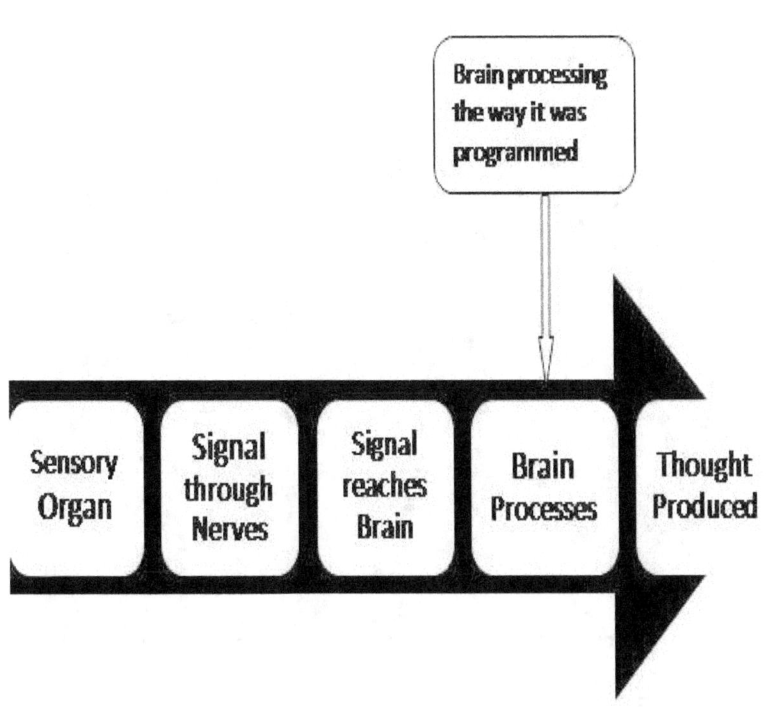

Brain processing the way it was programmed
Sensory Organ
Signal through Nerves
Signal reaches Brain
Brain Processes
Thought Produced

JUST BEE

Meditation class in Geneva Mar 2019

Meditation class in Brussels Apr 2019

CHAPTER – 3

KARMA

PURPOSE OF LIFE – ROLES & RESPONSIBILITIES

3.1 Karm is nothing but the roles and responsibilities we need to perform as defined and assigned by the social system for our co-existence in this society. Karm is the task we have to undertake, and these tasks should be performed optimally. For example, a car will perform optimally if it is properly tuned as per its specifications and is well serviced. If not, then it will give problems in meeting the expectations one has from owning and using a car. Same is the case for humans, for all their roles and responsibilities there are expectations from others towards whom the responsibilities have been assigned to us by this social system.

We all have been running full speed but have no clear idea about the purpose of life. Primarily, the purpose of life is to evolve as a good human being, and live peacefully, lovingly & happily. This is a common goal, but modern society has defined materialistic goals, which we all are chasing, leaving behind the core value and the core purpose. Unlike animals whose roles and purpose are very well defined and they do exactly that, we humans have been given the intelligence to evolve ourselves. So that we can perform even better and deliver better results.

3.2   Let us understand what roles and responsibilities do we get assigned when we grow up. Did we ever think about this? Probably not!

3.3   Various roles we take upon are of being a son, daughter, mother, father, cousin, neighbor, employee, manager, teacher, doctor, engineer, government employee, etc. In an organisation we create a job description for every role. Who creates a job description for humans in their social and personal roles? Literally no one. Were we told by our parents of our duties as a father or mother? Did we teach the same to our sons/daughters? Probably the answer remains a big NO.

3.4   Isn't it high time we sit and understand what all should have been our responsibilities for each role we have got assigned being part of this system we live in? This sounds weird but perhaps completely ignored during the upbringing of an individual. Perhaps it has lost its importance, as other materialistic goals have gained complete priority leaving no time for these teachings or introspection.

3.5   Once we have understood the roles and responsibilities, we will know how and what exactly is to be done every day in our life. Each role has a few tasks to be carried out on daily basis or at some other frequency of occurrence. The point is that we need to be focused on our tasks so that they are accomplished successfully and perfectly. We need to enjoy doing the tasks selflessly, without worrying about the outcome. Why without worrying about the outcome I will explain later as this might look incorrect right now. The mere fact is, that worrying is not needed. Moreover, here we are discussing peace of mind. Focus should be on doing it right and selflessly. Most tasks are for serving others.

3.6   Next is how to do, is based on the human design or Dharma or the law. Dharma or Human Design reflects the human characteristics of every human. If we are working at the best point of each characteristic, then every action of ours will be perfect, in the sense, every thought and action will generate happiness and there will be nothing that will trigger any negative thoughts in our mind.

3.7   If this can be achieved and our mind is constantly and consciously aware of this human system of operation, then there will never be conflicts in the mind as the mind is now aligned to the human design basis. Hence it will not have any negative thoughts as there are no negative actions or perceptions once you are aligned to your optimum characteristics.

3.8   Once we are able to operate at the optimum characteristics, we create a high-energy field that is positive. It elevates the body vibrations to a higher plane where the human perceptions also get elevated. At this stage, the energy created is also in alignment or in resonance with the internal soul and the external energy axis of the universe. When objects are in alignment and resonance they function amazingly and are always in harmony. Manifestations happen once in resonance with the creation. The creation helps to achieve what one sets out to achieve in life as part of roles and responsibilities.

3.9   Actions and plans are all about intentions and not expectations and results. The focus should be on tasks and its execution perfectly and not on the outcome. If we focus on the outcome then we lose focus on the execution, which will in turn trigger thoughts from expectations of outcomes. So we end up cluttering our mind. This is like making our lives complex unnecessarily.

3.10 Let's try and list the common roles and responsibilities and try to list the tasks associated with each role. This is not hard and fast, we are going to do this just for our understanding. One can do an introspection to redefine them again. Only thing is that when we are doing it, we should do it truthfully, sincerely, with an open mind, and without any ego.

For example, we can try to list down women's tasks in the following relationships. This may look a bit radical and will sound to be shocking as we may have never done this before. We may agree or disagree but the idea is to just try to list down our responsibilities towards various roles and relationships. These have to be really sincerely thought of without looking at others or comparing with others, else we will do injustice to ourselves.

3.10.1   **Parents** :

3.10.1.1   Take care of parent's health and daily needs if they need your support in achieving them. Depending on your age and situation there will be associated tasks. If you are 10 years old then you cannot have this task, but if you are, say 30 years or so, then you may have this as your task/responsibility to ensure that they get your morale, financial, and physical support whenever required. Maybe this will vary for each person and may not be applicable to all as every situation is different. Care has to be defined in each case. Help is not to be sought by the needy, but the giver has to identify what help is needed by the needy (mother in this case). Like when the mother looks after her child, she knows what is to be done and she does it selflessly with full love, passion, compassion, tirelessly, etc. We need to ask ourselves what needs to be done. Can you leave your parents helpless? If one cannot fully meet those commitments then one needs to see how best they can be managed within available resources, your capabilities and potential, and the circumstances. It is a very subjective thing to identify the tasks as each situation is pretty much unique.

3.10.1.2   Are you giving some time to spend with your parents? How often can you meet them and speak to them? How are you maintaining the bond and connectivity? Are you neglecting them?

3.10.1.3   What are their emotional needs and how can you meet them?

3.10.2   **Child**

3.10.2.1   How much time does your child need? Why?

3.10.2.2   How much time do you spend in conversation with your children?

3.10.2.3   Do you take them out for outings; play any outdoor games with them, or indoor board games.

3.10.2.4   Do they need your help as a teacher to improve them in some subjects if you can?

3.10.2.5   Are they getting enough exposure for their professional and vocational development?

3.10.2.6   Do you also talk to them about humanity, and how to be a good human?

3.10.2.7   Are your actions setting good examples for them?

3.10.2.8   Have you identified how can you educate your children and make them an independent person, well-educated so that they can be on their own emotionally and financially?

3.10.3 **Husband**

3.10.3.1   Are you able to cook for your husband or ensure the management of kitchen related tasks (under a scenario where the wife is a housewife/non-working)?

3.10.3.2   Are you not too demanding in terms of materialistic acquisitions?

3.10.3.3   Are you caring enough to see his needs?

3.10.3.4   Do you communicate well; spend enough time discussing personal, family as well as professional matters with him.

3.10.3.5   Are you flexible to adapt and mutually decide or are you imposing, and controlling?

3.10.3.6   Have you identified any other tasks to meet some more needs where you see he struggles or needs your support?

3.10.3.7   Are you an understanding person in times when he is stressed and needs to be heard?

3.10.3.8   Do you see areas where you need to take lead and guide him if he has a shortfall or lacks capability?

3.10.3.9   Are you discussing long-term and short-term plans together and are you both aligned with them.

3.10.3.10   Are you always there when he needs you or are you too busy outside with your own individuality.

3.10.3.11   Are you trying to push your tasks onto him in an unjustified and selfish way, without understanding his stress and professional workload and which may be beyond his capacity to undertake.

3.10.4   **Neighbours** :

3.10.4.1   What kind of relationships are you able to maintain with your neighbor?

3.10.4.2   Are you able to socialize with them?

3.10.4.3   Do you help them whenever there is a need within your capacity?

3.10.4.4   I hope that you are not doing something that causes problems for your neighbours.

3.10.5   **Relatives** (Aunts/Uncles/Cousins)

3.10.5.1   Are you a reason for cohesion and bonding with your relatives?

3.10.5.2   Are you communicating well and timely with your relatives?

3.10.5.3   Are you there in time of need for your relatives whenever it is possible?

3.11 In the case of man, most responsibilities above are almost similar except for the following below:-

3.11.1   Are you fulfilling your duties effectively so that you provide full protection and resources for the good and comfortable living for the family? Resources to impart good education for the children. Basically, a man's primary responsibility is to ensure that all logistics needs of the family are fulfilled by him through his job or business from a financial point of view, and other tasks from a service point of view. Many tasks in the house are co-managed by both husband and wife. Husband and wife complement each other in fulfilling the responsibilities of their family which primarily includes children and parents, in addition to relatives and friends who are a part of the social system we need to exist in.

Traditionally, the man was to manage the outside tasks and the breadwinner and the women the household. In today's time this has been completely mixed up and due to selfish motives has become a reason for discord between men and women. The changes in modern society have only made things worse. One can see where all this is leading the society to. There has been a constant degradation of society, relationships, and human value system.

3.12 Though I have tried to list down the roles and responsibilities here in short, but it is for us to truthfully see what my roles are, and what the associated responsibilities are. Before we deviate from these standard responsibilities and try to do something else, we should think responsibly and see how will it impact every individual in the family. Selfish motives and trying to shirk away primary responsibilities will ultimately create an imbalance in this old age well tested and proven social setup. It is our ego and other negative qualities that lead to this imbalance in the family set up by way of shirking of individual responsibilities. The gender bias created in society today is also leading to an imbalance in the system. Every change has to be systematically implemented in society but inside a house, rules are neither made nor followed. Now, this can be a long topic of discussion if we are not serious about understanding these. Without understanding these ourselves, we will never undertake and understand our roles and responsibilities correctly.

Many in today's younger generation are not even ready to undertake certain responsibilities. In fact they may not have been taught about their responsibilities when they enter into matrimonial alliances. They are also not willing to work hard and undertake many responsibilities like having children, they consider many responsibilities as a burden and try to avoid them. They have become more selfish and lazy, only looking for more materialistic comforts. The upbringings have become soft, filled with cushions and this does not make them a tough all-rounder.

These new changes in society have led to a general degradation in the family-based existence. Relationships turn sour and there is no fear of society's rules. Failed relationships ultimately lead to mental agony and depression and in the long run, one becomes a mental wreck.

I would say we are churning out a misguided and lost generation of children in today's world. Simple reason is that they have been brought up in a very easy way, and when they get ready to be on their own they succumb to pressures. They are unable to manage relationships as they are unable to handle responsibilities.

Therefore, the understanding of ROLES & RESPONSIBILITIES correctly without any bias truly is of utmost importance. Else people will simply exist on this planet without knowing their purpose.

CHAPTER – 4

DHARMA

HUMAN DESIGN

4.   WHAT IS HUMAN DESIGN AND WHY DO WE NEED TO UNDERSTAND

After understanding Karm we will now look into Dharm. (Though we spell Karma and Dharma, but it is pronounced as Karm and Dharm). There are three very important aspects that needs to be understood and are all interlinked

4.1   Human Design - Is there anything in this world that is created and has no purpose and has no unique design. If we want to understand ourselves then is it not necessary to know what our design basis is? How are we designed so that we can reach our objectives.

4.2   Purpose of Life - So the next question is, what is our purpose in life? What is the purpose of life? The purpose at a personal level, professional level and for self (internal) as well.

4.3   <u>How to achieve the purpose</u> – The last question is that if the purpose is known, then how do we achieve that or how do we operate to achieve our purpose.

4.4   The whole universe is nothing but consciousness and a flow of energy that is constantly getting transformed without getting destroyed or created. This has been proved even by modern science. Every creation maintains this logic while operating in this universe.

4.5   Everything created by the universe or even by humans has a specific purpose and a specific design according to the conceptualized purpose of the product. So how can we humans be different from each other, intrinsically we are all equal only. Has anyone even bothered to think about what the design or the characteristics of humans is and what should be the purpose?

4.6   In my understanding the purpose is to realize who we are, how should we exist and perform our tasks, and whatever tasks we happen to be assigned. What is this mortal body and what is the immortal soul inside? How are we one with the consciousness or the ever prevalent energy of the cosmos?

4.7   Therefore, it is important to understand the HUMAN DESIGN or the human characteristics. We will now see which all human qualities can be listed so that we can introspect and check ourselves with respect to these qualities. Once we check where we do stand with respect to each of these qualities we will know what all needs to be corrected as far as each one of us is concerned. Once we identify our flaws or the negative qualities we will have to raise our awareness so that these negative qualities are removed by consistent effort and consistent awareness. If we are not even aware of these negative qualities then how will we make an effort to remove them. We can only change ourselves and we cannot change others. Yes, we can always inspire others. Changing ourselves by realizing our own flaws and making corrections is what is needed. Anything wrong needs correction for optimal performance as per the design. Therefore, constantly looking for flaws in order to improve performance is a simple logic to be applied even to ourselves, by every individual. If we are able to achieve 100% success in transforming ourselves into pure human beings, then that will be the moment of self-realization or enlightenment. At that moment you will achieve total bliss, complete peace of mind, and a steady meditative state of existence.

4.8 By making changes in the way we perceive everything and by changing the negative qualities to the positive ones, we will get rid of all the negative thoughts. **All negative qualities are the reason for triggering negative thoughts**. Once we know this trick to make the necessary changes in ourselves, we can practice and execute this process of transformation. This is the process and this is what needs to be practiced gradually which will eventually bring in the required change in us. Ultimately, liberating our mind from the onslaught of the evil thoughts, which were earlier triggered by our negative qualities. **Peace of mind will emerge.**

HUMAN DESIGN – HUMAN MIRROR

S	Qualities	1	2	3	4	5	6	7	8	9	10
1	No Ego										
2	Truthfulness										
3	Selfless										
4	Patient										
5	Not Comparing										
6	Not Jealous										
7	Generous										
8	Caring										
9	Compassion										
10	Passion										
11	Hard Working										
12	Responsible										
13	Tolerant										
14	No Anger										
15	No greed										
16	Detached										
17	No Expectation										
18	No Hatred										
19	Loving unconditio										
20	Sacrificing										
21	Forgiving										
22	Kind										
23	Destiny believer										
24	Not Controlling										
25	Accept Mistakes										
26	Trusting										
27	Fearless										
28	Confident										
29	Not Calculative										
30	Logical										
31	Quick Decision										
32	Joy of Giving										

33	Simplicity												
34	Austerity												
35	Grounded												
36	No Lust												
37	Acceptance												
38	Surrendering												
39	Empathy												
40	Not manipulative												
41	Letting Go												
42	Not Possessive												
43	Organised												
44	Neat & Hygienic												
45	No Desires												
46	Not harmful												
47	Gratitude												

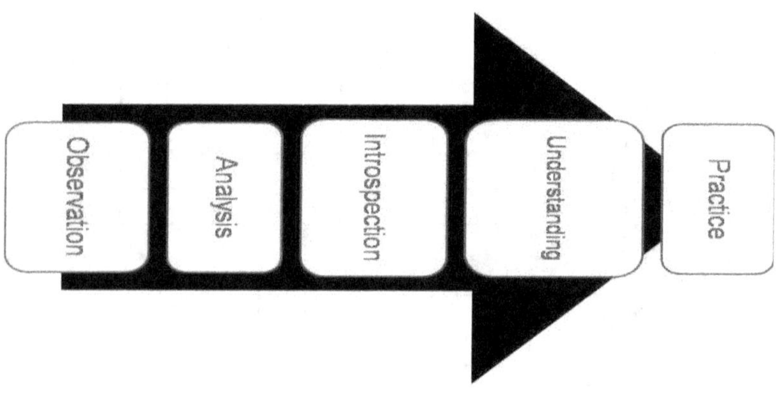

4.8 The human mirror lists all the possible core human qualities or human characteristics as well as associated or secondary human qualities. This can be discussed in detail with daily life examples. What is needed here is a process that is depicted in the diagram above. This process is nothing but a practice of constant or regular Contemplation. This is also known as SADHANA. Sadhana is a Hindi word for practice and this is a popular word in the world of spirituality in India.

4.9 We will have to follow this process for each of these human qualities to identify how it is tuned in ourselves. We should use the score sheet to mark ourselves on the scorecard. 10 being the most positive quality, and 0 being the most negative quality scores. Once we are truthfully able to judge ourselves with respect to these qualities and get our score, then we have a task in front of us to work on to start improving our score. So raised awareness is needed for every thought and action. A constant contemplation is needed or if not constant at least get some time out in a day to do some introspection about the day's thoughts and actions to find out whether any of the negative qualities have impacted your thoughts and actions or not. By capturing these we are able to give feedback to the brain so that the next time the brain uses this feedback before processing similar events. Every time the brain uses the feedback it allows one to provide a decision to the brain to remove the negative quality and use the positive side of it. **Through repeated efforts over a period of time, the pattern or the programming of the brain will change from an erstwhile negative quality to a positive quality**. This way we can tackle each of the negative qualities and turn them into positive qualities. As the changes happen or begin you will notice the gradual onset of peace in your mind, thereby, getting released from all negative thoughts and worries. Ultimately making you reach a consistently happy state of mind. THIS IS WHAT IS CALLED **SADHANA** or Practice, finally leading to liberation.

We will discuss a few of the human qualities here so that you can get an idea of how to understand each quality, and its meaning, and then the process of introspection and contemplation, to understand the flaw in you, and then the practice of changing that. Once the whole process is understood, then it is up to you how to change oneself and how much and how sincerely to put an effort.

Just to remind us and always keep in our mind that, here we have been constantly discussing **KARMA** and **DHARMA**.

4.9.1   **JEALOUSY :** Let us take Jealousy as the first example. What is Jealousy? When we get unhappy to see others happy or getting successful. Jealousy gives the feeling of sadness, unhappiness, and even hatred. So ultimately getting jealous is harmful to one's own self.   It is like a self-inflicted injury. Jealousy comes when we are selfish and want everything for ourselves and we want to prove that we are better than others. There is a sort of comparison and competition, which is not a healthy competition. So it is the ego which makes you compare, compete and make you feel that you are not equal but superior. So jealousy is due to these negative qualities ingrained during your upbringing. Upbringing, because during the formative years, whatever we see and get influenced by, we accept them as the norm, and imbibe them into our lives.

Any thought arising out of any input from the sensory organs if it gives unhappiness than that is not a good way to perceive things. We should recognize this and change our way of thinking knowing that this is giving us unhappiness. Also, logically thinking, why should one get unhappy to see others prosper. Everyone is reaping the benefits of their work (Karmas) past and present and that is what their destiny through this karmic cycle becomes. If we get happiness in seeing a prospering society, then not only will we get happiness, but also inspiration. All good things are meant to inspire us and teach us and make us progress in life.

Once we understand deeply that it is not good to be jealous then we can start to block those thoughts, and later they will stop getting triggered. This regular introspection of all instances of getting thoughts filled with jealousy will tell us that these thoughts have become an obstacle in our pursuit of happiness. Then only we will start tackling them and avoiding them. The thought of not getting jealous will send feedback to the brain and every time the thought of jealousy is getting generated the brain will always give feedback before generating the thought of jealousy. With this interlock, we will be able to instruct the brain to not generate such thoughts of jealousy. Thus the pattern of processing will change and gradually one will get out of the pattern of getting jealous and slowly the pattern will change to happiness in such events.

This transformation will start becoming evident as the happiness one receives makes a perceptible difference in one's life. The beginning of the change with the arrival of happiness will become a motivation and a driving force, coupled by the will power and self-control, the practice will increase the speed of transformation. The grace of the universe will arrive as well, when one has made good progress.

Introspection can be done when one gets some quiet time in one's daily routine. You will have to make this a routine to find time to do introspection. Otherwise living without introspection and wasting time in useless things like mobile phones, Television, gossiping, etc will take your life in the other direction of unhappiness and mental instability. Even better is if one can take time off and visit quiet places surrounded by nature like mountains, riversides, lakes, forests, parks, etc. Nature helps in removing distractions and allows one to do a more peaceful introspection. That is why the majority of spiritual seekers and yogis ultimately move towards nature and start residing there. Why does nature provide such solace, because nature is primarily a giver and while amidst nature we are not having any expectations from nature. We know that nature gives unconditionally. In the material world, we are always expecting and unsure of the externalities.

We saw jealousy and its impact on mind and then how to change it through introspection and awareness. Then practicing the change of perception creation in real time living. Similarly, we can see the same process of transformation for the other human qualities.

4.9.2   **EGO** : Let us understand ego. Ego is something that prevents you from finding the truth and makes you live a life like a big fool. A person with a bigger ego is a bigger stupid and is actually fooling his/her own self. He/she becomes an ignorant person, covered by the darkness due to ignorance. Ego keeps a person in darkness. The egoistic person thinks no end of himself/herself. The egoistic person thinks that he/she is perfect, most successful, and most knowledgeable. The egoistic person wants to constantly portray that he/she is perfect, knowledgeable, and successful. Psychologically, it feels that the egoistic person is carrying a superiority complex, but in reality the person is suffering from an inferiority complex. Therefore, such a person is constantly trying to portray an image of being a superior person. It is said that, ego is inversely proportional to knowledge. The lesser the knowledge, the higher is the ego.

Though the egoistic person is actually aware of his/her flaws or whatever is lacking in them, but he/she fails to acknowledge or accept them. This causes a constant internal conflict the person gets into with his/her own self. This conflict leads to constant manipulation so as to portray oneself as a superior person. This leads to the triggering of other negative qualities which in turn trigger multiple negative thoughts. Therefore, ego keeps triggering negative thoughts. Ego makes one person believe that he/she knows everything thus keeping such a person ignorant and unknowledgeable, effectively in darkness about the realities of life. Due to a lack of knowledge, the person makes repeated mistakes and subsequently triggering a loss of self-confidence. Mistakes made due to ego result in negative thoughts arising out of failures and expectations of not being able to achieve something. It then leads to fears of failing to portray an image of being a successful person materialistically.

The most important thing about ego is that it prevents a person to look at their own mistakes and flaws thereby hindering their personal development as a good human being. Such a person is actually preventing his/her own transformation. Such a person will always be filled with negative thoughts arising out of superiority and inferiority complexes, comparison, jealousy, selfishness, expectations, desires, and many more interlinked human qualities. It is most difficult to be aware of one's own ego. Therefore, a real deeper introspection is needed to analyse the presence of ego in our thoughts and actions. Then with raised awareness catch those negative thoughts and start preventing them from attacking your mind.

4.9.3 **DESIRELESS** : What are desires and what are needs. One needs to understand that there is a difference between needs and desires. In life, we should work for our needs and not unwanted desires. Every desire which is beyond the needs based on our roles and responsibilities can be considered as an unwanted desire. Desires based on greed, selfishness, and lust are going to cause constant and consistent misery, by generating a constant barrage of negative thoughts. I am sure that no one needs to teach us that being selfish, having lust and greed are not good qualities to possess. So it is important to understand their impact on our mind. Desires create expectations, and then the effort required to fulfill such desires itself takes a toll on one's life and peaceful existence. One has to probably compromise with one's responsibilities and re-prioritize the unwanted desires over the real needs, therefore, causing an unwanted imbalance in one's life. When such desires are not met then it leads to thoughts of frustration, followed by thoughts of anger and anxiety, maybe depressive thoughts of failures and loss of self-confidence. Therefore, unwanted desires can lead to many other triggers culminating in many negative thoughts. Introspection is required to understand what the actual needs are and what unwanted desires are. One can have intentions but not expectations. Also, all needs should be built around one's roles and responsibilities. Roles and responsibilities are the originators of our tasks or karmas. If one wants to go beyond the needs, then one should question oneself. Are these coming out of greed and lust?

For every unwanted desire, there is an effort required and for all the unwanted effort there is also time and energy required. One might try to manipulate to achieve such desires and all these actions can lead to the constant creation of negative thoughts. Thought of fear may also arise if one is worried about the desire not getting fulfilled. So effectively this is a vicious whirlpool one can unknowingly and surreptitiously get into.

Many unwanted desires put us on a runway which can lead to burnout and unhappiness and losing whatever we had also achieved. People chasing materialistic things end up losing the basic things which would have given them happiness. While on such a runway we start losing friends and family, as distances are created. As one does not have the time for the family itself, while chasing unwanted desires of acquiring materialistic success.

This is a long discussion as almost every human quality gets interlinked here with the creation of unwanted desires. Ego one of them as one also wants to create a superiority complex by showing that I am better than others and more successful, a false identity we all are trying to create constantly. I have acquired more than you.

So unwanted desires arise out of a mixture of many negative qualities, and then they trigger many other interlinked negative thoughts. A real deeper introspection is required here as well, to make the change - the transformation in oneself.

While writing a book and explaining through writing many times it is not completely possible to explain or convey clearly to everyone the concept and the meaning. Therefore, verbal communication is always better. The best is self-discovery and self-exploration.

SATSANG – a company of wise people or in fact saints that can bring in the required change. Satsang means in the company of good people, wise people. In Indian philosophy, a regular Satsang has been given high importance in people's lives.

4.9.4   **SELFLESS :** Is it good to be selfish or selfless? Should our actions and thoughts be selfish or selfless? I am sure if we all ask ourselves truthfully we will all give the same answer, that we should be selfless. From inside we all know what is right and what is wrong, it is only because of our ego and external influences we might give a different answer or partially agree and disagree.

While doing introspection a good approach is to ask pertinent questions to your own self. Like, will selfless actions/karma give us happiness or selfish karma? Selfless karma is focused on the positive outcome of karma so it is not filled with expectations for selfish desires. Selfless karmas are always directed toward the benefit of others. If karmas are our duties and responsibilities based on our various roles, then all responsibilities are primarily for others. Primarily each individual is taken care of by others' actions. Therefore, in this system of family and community of humans, the needs are fulfilled by others. Effectively we are all working for fulfilling the needs of our community, families, and organizations. Similarly, we work for an organization and the organization pays us a salary. If we are doing a business then we are actually providing products or services to others, in turn, we get paid for the products or services provided. In each of these actions, if we focus on the joy of giving to others through the actions of producing products or services, the end user will be happy and their happiness will actually give us real happiness.

If we become selfish and start thinking only about our own greed and selfish desires, then in every action we will shift our focus towards our greed, desires, and lust instead of the quality of product or services, thereby, affecting the quality of service and ultimately leading to an unhappy end customer. Subsequently, a loss of face and loss of trust towards the end user. Eventually, giving you unhappiness. Greed shifts the focus to acquiring more materialistically and going beyond one's needs. Thereby chasing unwanted desires, and creating unrealistic expectations instead of good intentions. Further, this leads to a manipulative way of working and trying to control the outcome by unethical means. Frustration results when the unwieldy desires are not met, leading to bitterness and anger. So it is a chain reaction of negative tendencies leading to many negative thoughts and ultimately losing peace of mind. The whole point is that the focus shifted from karma to unwanted targets and methods. So the primary objective is lost resulting in self-destruction of mental peace. None of us realize that we are harming ourselves by being selfish.

4.9.5   DESTINY : (Understanding destiny), It is very important to understand what is DESTINY. Without understanding destiny, one cannot understand the entire inter-connection between these human qualities. There is actually nothing random in this universe or nothing like being fortunate. The whole creation has to be scientific. There has to be an order and rule for the cosmos to operate. For example, if we look at the earth or planets in the solar system, they are rotating around their axis at a fixed speed which never changes conspicuously. They are revolving around the sun in their fixed orbits from time immemorial. So many natural phenomena one can see indicate that everything has been scientifically designed to operate. Nothing is random. If there was randomness, then imagine what will happen to this world. See the birds, they are all hard-wired to operate, so they are living in cohesion with nature, they sleep at a fixed time; they follow fixed patterns, etc. Flora, it is all fixed based on weather and climate.

If we look around and do such observations and introspection about this beautiful creation of the creator, then only we will realize how the creation is operating unceasingly, uninterrupted, until and unless humans tinkered with nature.

Then nature retorts as per the law of creation to create a balance.

Therefore, it is logically good to understand that every outcome of every action of every human is bound to create a result that will be according to an individual's act, or karma. Good karma will lead to good results and bad karma will lead to bad results. As we did discuss earlier that humans are no different and they are created to operate as humans and not as inhuman. So what is humanity? It is being a good person. This is said emotionally, but scientifically it is a fact that all humans are supposed to operate as per the law of nature. Here we call it DHARMA. If we are operating as per the Dharma then all our actions will yield positive results. It is the outcome of every karma, which creates our destiny. Destiny is a constant happening in our life based on our past actions/karma. Our past karma from this birth and past births results in our present destiny and our present actions will create our future destiny.

No one else is responsible for our destiny except for us.

There is a way to dissolve the negative outcome of the past bad karma if we realize that we did some mistake in our thoughts and actions, thereby repenting and truly seeking forgiveness and then ensuring that such mistakes are not repeated.

Life is a journey and when we make mistakes it is important to understand that we need to ensure that the same mistakes are not repeated again. This is generally a natural tendency when we realize in any situation that a mistake was made and that we make the necessary course correction.

When a ship is sailing, the course it has to chart is being set up in the navigation system. Whenever there is a deviation in the course, the feedback system gives a signal for the required course correction.

As humans we are nothing more than a device or a machine. The only difference is that in humans there is this option given to take a decision, good or bad. So we need to be aware of our actions so as to ensure that we are on the right course.

Therefore, it is very important to do regular introspection on DESTINY, so that we understand it really well. The conclusion is, that everything is happening at a given time and space, and as per destiny, which is being created out of our own actions. Only with this understanding our introspection and conclusions will be correct while doing introspection.

All the human qualities which we collectively call DHARMA or one can call human design, or Human Rule Book, or Human Specifications, or Human Operating Parameters, have to be very well understood. In understanding each of the qualities we need to understand every interlinked quality.

I can go on explaining and giving examples after examples but it is for you to do this exploration yourself.

Another example, none of us knows how our life unfolds. We can also not predict what will happen in the future. Though we all try hard to control it, most of us have no idea about our future. Therefore, it is easy to say that life unfolds as per our karmas and destiny. So it is destiny in other words. The whole point is that one needs to focus on one's KARMAs and perform them as per the DHARMA.

4.9.6 **TOLERANCE** : Tolerance or Patience. Both are almost similar with a very subtle difference. What exactly is tolerance? Do we acknowledge that everything happens when the time is right and if it is destined to happen? Therefore, one should again remain focused on the action rather than its outcome. Intention to achieve any goal is needed and not expectation. Expectations lead to worries even before the result is arrived at or when the result turns unfavourable. So destiny and time are the factors to be kept in mind or to be aware of, which will provide tolerance or rather patience for any outcome to happen. Otherwise, intolerance and impatience will give rise to worries or negative thoughts which will again trigger many other negative qualities and therefore many more negative thoughts. Tolerance differs slightly from patience in some instances, as an example, if we do not like something or someone, it may be just the presence of someone around us or some place, but we have to accept that situation and let it be, so that is tolerance. Literally, nothing is under our control and happens as per the law of karma and as desired or planned by the universe or God. Therefore, we have to let the events unfold around us even if they are not favourable, and also we are not in a position to make any difference to those events. If we can tolerate all externalities in this illusive world, then our mind will remain inert and unperturbed by those events. That means we learn to be neutral to everything good or bad. Especially, bad or unfavourable, or not to our liking. Neutrality, destiny, time, and karma are all interlinked for the understanding of tolerance. Basically, the need to be tolerant is our ability to remain neutral to all the externalities while being aware of destiny and acceptance of the outcomes. Then only we can have our peace of mind. Here I have covered both patience and tolerance in one paragraph. Like we have to be patient enough for things to happen in their due course of time and be able to tolerate the time factor in getting to the outcome. Therefore, once we realize the ill effects of intolerance and impatience, we can start to change our way of thinking and perceptions, and reactions. Thereby transforming this particular quality and subsequently eliminating another cause of negative thoughts.

If we are not tolerant then we can also become impulsive. At minor disagreements or dislikes, we might lose our temperament and get angry and then misbehave, thereby, causing friction even in the relationships. Big egos lead to intolerance and impulsiveness because we don't want to change ourselves and our ego tells us that stay on your egoistic path. Instability of mind due to many factors like multiple failures also makes a person impulsive. The present generation is very impulsive as they have higher expectations and are totally gripped by materialism and a desire for quick achievement of their materialistic goals.

4.9.7 **DETACHMENT** : This is another very important quality or rather the penultimate goal in one's spiritual progress. In the Hindi language, it is also called Vairagya. Vairagya means mentally renouncing this illusionary world. Then only one can live in this world with peace, being detached to everything physical and visible. Attachments are a cause of misery because we assume ownership of material and other physical possessions including humans – (friends and relatives or family or peers, subordinates, etc). When the expectations are not fulfilled, then the attachments due to the possessiveness or ownership create expectations and control, leading to frustration and anger. Attachments also in a way create mental baggage or burden we carry in our mind constantly.

It is important to understand that we don't own anything in this world. Everything we need is just to fulfill our basic needs till the time needs exist. Needs change with time but people don't let go or give away what is not needed. Accumulation is the result of attachment and greed and possessiveness, even ego of ownership and feeling of being superior.

Everything in this world is transient and ever-changing, so nothing will stay on permanently. Therefore, getting attached leads to pain and worldly suffering, especially when the time comes to part with the attached material or beings.

Like death is inevitable but we cry or have sorrow when parting happens with the near and dear ones as if they were here to be with us forever.

Attachments should not be confused with love and care. Loving anyone should be a natural thought and action, care is an essential ingredient of every action and thought. So attachment and detachment have no relation to being loving or caring. The focus should be on performing one's karmas/roles and responsibilities.

Any thought which makes us unhappy needs to be checked that such thoughts are unwanted. If we remain un-attached and fulfill our duties and responsibilities perfectly, sincerely, and lovingly, you will realize that everything remains beautiful with no suffering. No negative thoughts.

Attachments to people, material possessions, and the accumulation of materialistic possessions all lead to suffering when there are changes occurring in these possessions. For example, if one is attached to one's parents and when the relationship with our parents turns sour with time, then this will make one suffer emotionally/mentally. We are so used to these attachments with people and material that it is very difficult to understand and live and practice detachment with everything. We have to constantly remind ourselves that we came alone in this world and will depart alone. Therefore, we should be living alone mentally without being attached to anything. Life is all about fulfilling our duties/responsibilities. Logically we are alone, though physically we appear to be with other physical beings and objects which is all very transient. Transient sources cannot be a constant source of happiness because they themselves are transient.

If we cannot get detached, then mind will not be able to get rid of negative thoughts arising out of unfavorable events resulting from the attachments.

So it is of utmost importance to understand what detachment is, and its impact on our minds.

We get attached to our status, position in society, position in the organization, position in the family, and the false sense of respect that comes from these artificial or temporary positions and identities. This leads to suffering, when the temporary phases of life go through changes, especially when one loses these positions or possessions due to whatever reason.

All the social identities are based on money and status. All such identities are artificial and temporary. Constant effort is needed to sustain these artificial identities. This itself creates many negative thoughts which dissipate our energy due to the constant onslaught of negative thoughts arising out of this misery. The so called respect one feels one is getting is also artificial and is there till one is in possession of such materialistic things or status. People's attitudes towards us change when the status changes, thereby, proving that all these transactions were fake. We have built a society around fake materialistic identities. If you want real happiness then embrace the real truth and ignore and detach from the fake social, illusionary, materialistic, the ever transient consumerist world around us. Just focus on duties and responsibilities or Karma. Do the karma diligently, intelligently, sincerely, lovingly, and selflessly, and you will remain eternally happy, like being in a meditative state.

4.9.8 **CARING** : It is not difficult to understand how being caring is a positive quality and how does it provide happiness. Just ask yourself if you are not caring then how will this affect you in accomplishing your roles and responsibilities properly. Eventually, not being able to provide effectively what one has to provide to the end user through your responsibilities and duties. Thereby, depriving them of what you were expected to provide. Ultimately making them unhappy and in return, you can never be happy. Care is an essential ingredient in every thought and action, and it makes the other person happy when you are always caring and taking care of them. It is also your responsibility as a good human being to be always caring irrespective of whether the other person is reciprocating or not. Others are responsible for their actions and we need to stay unattached and neutral to others actions. We can only ensure that our own actions are as per the rule book - Dharma. The problem comes when we start to expect based on our deeds that we have been good to them, but they are not doing or fulfilling their responsibilities towards us. This imbalance leads to trying to do tit for tat and then starts a never ending friction in the relationships.

If everyone in this world followed the Dharma then there will be just love and harmony everywhere. As this world is ever changing, and perfect becomes imperfect, and sometimes imperfect becomes perfect. Therefore, we should remain inert to these externalities and stay focused on our tasks unattached. Then only we can remain happy. All negative thoughts, sadness, sufferings are generated when we are looking for happiness from these externalities. A changing, fluctuating source of happiness cannot provide constant happiness if the source itself is changing and is also temporary.

4.9.9   **TRUTHFULNESS : **Is it good to always speak the truth, except for some exceptional circumstances strategically, which will ensure that the situation is not causing any harm to the other. Though one should avoid such situations where one has to strategically cover the truth diplomatically. Barring this exception, one should always speak the truth. Though once you go deeper in this transformation you will acknowledge that there is no need to speak a lie in any situation. What happens when one speaks a lie? How does a lie trigger negative thoughts? Truth consolidates trust between two people. Trust is very important between humans for harmony, love, and cohesion. Once a lie is spoken there is always a fear of the truth getting revealed. This constant fear of getting exposed causes a constant generation of negative thoughts. Nature has created humans in such a way that no individual can go against the law of nature created for humans. Humans can never get larger than the creator. Sometimes to cover a lie, one ends up speaking more lies, making the whole situation even more harmful for the person speaking these lies.

One who speaks the truth will always sleep peacefully as there is nothing to hide for him/her. The person who always speaks the truth will therefore have no negative thoughts due to being truthful. A truthful person is considered to be the most trustworthy person. Without trust, the co-existence is on a shaky ground.

So we can easily see how being truthful prevents the occurrence of negative thoughts and keeps the mind free. We can discuss these things endlessly and brainstorm them to come to a converging conclusion, which is nothing different from the truth – the absolute truth.

4.9.10 **Not having HATRED :** Question oneself, what happens when we develop hatred? A dislike leads to hatred. Hatred is a stronger negative quality as compared to the quality of dislike. If we develop hatred towards a person then this negative quality will always generate intense negative thoughts in one's mind. Loving all generates happiness and no negative thoughts. Hatred comes when one is comparing oneself with others, and is not happy when seeing others progress or be happy in life. Hatred comes when we feel that we are superior to others and deny the co-existence of all beings. Hatred comes from being selfish also. So the initial negative qualities which trigger hatred are comparison, ego, and selfishness.

The positive quality to be possessed is love and the opposite of this is hatred. Therefore, it is said that treat all equally and accept everyone around us as equal. Understand that this world is like one big family, so love all unbiased and unconditionally. The thoughts and actions filled with love will spread happiness in others and in return will generate happiness in you. There is no better happiness than seeing others happy. Though most people in today's world behave the other way around.

4.9.11 **GENEROSITY** : Is being generous good or not being generous good? Asking these questions sincerely to yourself will give you the right answer. If you start using your ego and the polluted mind then you might give a different answer. Here we are discussing the mind and its complete purification so that it is liberated from all negative thoughts and reaches a state of bliss. There should be no middle path.

Why are people not generous? This is what needs to be understood and once we understand the reason then only we realize that we always need to be generous in our thoughts and actions. Generosity is also linked to sacrifices. We also say, "Service before self", or selfless service for others. This was taught in the military, and I had worked in the Indian Navy, so I remember this. Though this is applicable to every individual.

Generosity is enacted in many ways. One can give time, money, and any other support whenever it is possible within your capacity. Just the thought of helping someone itself is good enough as practically it may not be possible to enact every time an act of generosity. Generosity gives the ultimate Joy of Giving. We need to keep in mind that it is always the intentions that matter. Every action should be filled with thoughts of generosity, care, compassion, empathy etc. Every action (karma) is part of one's roles and responsibilities towards others. So generosity is inevitably a good quality to have.

ALL OF THE ABOVE 40 PLUS QUALITIES MENTIONED HERE ARE NECESSARY INGREDIENTS IN EVERY THOUGHT AND ACTION FOR THE COMBINED BENEFIT OF THE HUMANITY. EVERY THOUGHT AND ACTION HAS THE PRESENCE OF ALL THESE QUALITIES, SO IT IS IMPORTANT TO UNDERSTAND THE PRESENCE OF ALL THESE IN EVERY THOUGHT AND ACTION. LOVE IS THE BASIS OF OUR EXISTENCE IN EVERY THOUGHT AND ACTION, AND LOVE IS A COMBINED EFFECT OF ALL THESE POSITIVE HUMAN QUALITIES. THAT IS WHAT THE TRUE UNCONDITIONAL LOVE IS.

4.9.12 **HARMLESS** : One should always be helpful and always ensure that every action of ours does not cause any harm to the other person in any situation. If an action causes any harm to the other person(s), then the effect of the harm will make that doer unhappy as well and result in own sufferings. As we dwell into each and every human characteristic, we realize that impact of each has to be thoroughly analysed to understand what is going wrong with our thoughts and actions which are being generated based on the tuning of these human qualities in us. If most qualities are tuned to act negatively then we will have a constant flooding of negative thoughts. No technique in this world can change the condition of your mind. No Guru can do any magic trick. A Guru's grace is showered only when an individual is making sincere efforts to transform oneself through this practice of finding own flaws and then injecting the necessary corrections.

4.9.13   **COMPASSION** : What if we are not compassionate towards others. This can make us nonchalant with respect to what is happening around us. Happiness cannot come in a society if there is an imbalance in society. Collectively there has to be a cohesive existence, in harmony and with equality. A community or a country cannot progress and citizens cannot be happy if there is an imbalance in the society, socially and economically. Without compassion, we will isolate ourselves and ultimately result in living unhappily. The ego of trying to prove one's superiority over others also results in not being compassionate. Selfishness also leads to not being compassionate.

I am sure by now you know how to first analyse and understand each of these qualities and then check their impact on our mind.

4.9.14 **NO EXPECTATIONS** : What is expectation? Why do we generate or create expectations? What happens when expectations are not met? How do we react when expectations are not met? Why should we not have expectations? These are a few of the questions one needs to ask oneself.

So here we need to remember that whatever we do or others do, there is always an element of destiny. Everything happens based on past karmas or destiny. Therefore, what is required is to focus on karma and having good intentions of completing the task sincerely with love and care and hard work, so that the result is beneficial for the end recipient. If the favourable result is destined to happen then one will have favourable result, and if unfavourable result is destined to happen then come what may be and whatever effort one can make, the result will be unfavourable. So one should remain neutral to the outcome of efforts and karmas, whether it is self-karmas or other's karmas. If we focus on expectations then there is always an element of fear and uncertainty, there can also be anxiety, nervousness, panic, frustration, anger, lack of confidence, depression, etc. Instead, if in every action the focus is on performing the karmas correctly, then we will enjoy the karma. Focus on karma means that the karma is performed with sincerity, love, diligence, and selflessly so that the best effort is made. Then there is happiness while performing the karma as there is focus without any distractions from the expectations. It also ensures that no other negative qualities will get triggered to generate negative thoughts. Even if the outcome is not favourable the end recipients know that you made sincere efforts. So it is the response of the end recipient about the outcome of the karma which gives happiness in return. We should also remember that we all learn from mistakes. If there were mistakes and one could realize those mistakes made during the execution, then one can try again with a different approach or solution. Sometimes external factors are also not favourable and one has to let go. **Acceptance** is important.

Here I would give another example of any family where there are 2-3 children. The effort from the parents is almost the same so as to ensure a good future for their children. We see that all the three children do differently. Sometimes some children fair very badly in life, while some do exceptionally well. So it is their individual destiny that takes them on their life's journey. Parents are just a medium through which life takes form on earth again as humans and then they continue on their own paths of their individual souls. Parents, who don't understand this, suffer lifelong when their children don't turn up as per their expectations. Had they focused on their karma of being a parent rather than expectations they would have not suffered from the misery of their expectations. Every individual has their own destiny.

I hope you understand how having expectations trigger negative thoughts and it also leads to other negative triggers leading to more negative thoughts.

4.9.15   **NO LUST** : Lust is a form of greed. Lust can be there for materialistic things as well as physical (sexual). Generally, lust is used when it is a greed for sex. Though, the thought of having unwanted desires is also called lust or greed. We have already discussed what desires are and what basic needs are. Why should there be no lust? This is a deep topic. What does lust do to our mind? We also need to understand pure love and how it is different from lust. The problem is that we identify ourselves with the physical body. Lust is the biggest distraction created in this illusionary world. Sex is the biggest illusion and we get completely distracted by it. Each person has a different level of lust in them, depending upon their upbringing and exposure. When we identify ourselves with the physical body then we are completely immersed in this illusion. We need to identify every living being with their souls, what we call inner beauty. Knowing that there is inner beauty we get attracted to or rather distracted towards the external looks and appearances. This is the charm created by this materialistic and illusionary world. The pleasures we feel we will get though the fulfillment of lust are momentary and cannot be there constantly. We are discussing about the constant state of peace of mind, and therefore we need to eliminate the sources of happiness, which are transient.

If this is clear then only we will start getting aware of thoughts arising out of lust and the immoral actions resulting from that. Can sex or thoughts resulting from lust give us eternal constant happiness? If that was the case people would be just following that and would have reached a state of permanent bliss, but that is not the case. More lust and more instability of mind, in the end, one is searching forever? In short, one is always wandering and can become a predator. Forever worried and unhappy, it is actually, a deflection of one's mind to a wrong and an illusionary target. A person loses the right path and forgets where the real source of all-pervasive happiness is. Lust is an extreme form of unwanted desire, which if not fulfilled generates negative thoughts and if fulfilled may provide momentary pleasures. The constant effort, manipulation, etc to fulfill the lust also creates havoc in the mind. So we need to understand this beast called lust which actually haunts us lifelong and plays havoc with our mind. The choice is ours Lust or inner happiness. Beauty or the Beast !

4.9.16 **NO GREED**: We will try to understand what greed is, and its impact on the mind. Greed here is more so for desiring materialistic things. The urge to acquire more than needed is Greed. Therefore, again it is required to understand what needs are and what desires are. If one aspires to acquire something which is more than the basic need then one has to accept that there has to be more time and effort needed to achieve those and then one should not be compromising the other basic needs. Basic needs can be like giving enough time to the family or having a work life balance. Therefore, again it is important to understand what are the roles and responsibilities one has, and what are the needs according to these roles and responsibilities. Acquiring more than the needs can also have an adverse impact on the upbringing of the children. One should also analyse, whether it is really needed to have such acquisitions. How will they add to the happiness in your life? Aren't most materialistic acquisitions just a provider of momentary pleasures, or rather impulsive pleasures or satisfaction? Are we compromising on something to meet these unwanted desires? One can always try to justify these desires if you use your ego and mind. Does the size of a house decide how much happy will a person be? Are people living in large houses more happy? One should understand rightfully what kind of house is needed for the family based on family size etc. Once the need is defined then one has to work towards it. Therefore, it is very important to truthfully define needs and differentiate between needs and desires. The Gap between them is what Greed is. This greed creates an unknown unwanted target being chased by you, which eventually creates unhappiness. It is so due to the various side effects of the whole effort involved in fulfilling those desires borne out of greed. This is a deep topic and difficult to write everything in a connected flowing way. In short, GREED puts us on the highway to burnout and unhappiness. So recognize the greed in your nature and understand how will it create worries in your life. Life is all about peace of mind and nothing else.

4.9.17 **TRUSTING** : What happens if we do not trust. Trust is between two people, trust is also having belief in destiny, God, etc. Here one has to understand everything logically. I am not saying anything and asking you to believe it. We should deliberate over every word through logical and analytical thinking. If everyone behaves perfectly and humanity is at its best it is easy to trust. Unfortunately in today's world, most people are behaving worldly so trust has weaned out. But if we start on a no trust note then the way ahead will not be good. We need to act right irrespective of others' thoughts and actions or intentions, because everyone pays for their karma. We have to remember that our karmas are not based on other's karmas. Now, this can be debated in certain conditions, like if someone betrays repeatedly then how should you behave. So on a case-to-case basis, one can analyse, but in genera,l one should always make a beginning with trust.

Now, what happens if there is no trust, our thoughts will be filled with uncertainty and anxiety. There will be no love between two people and the whole exchange will be a formal transaction based on manipulation and shrewdness. This will obviously not give rise to good thoughts but only negative thoughts. Therefore, from our side, we should begin on trust. Sometimes, unknowingly things don't turn favourable and we assume that the other person did something wrong and on this assumption, we lose trust. Not trusting has become a common disease in this selfish and materialistic world.

ASSUMING is a big disease in most of us. We always assume without knowing the reality and mostly the assumptions turn out to be wrong. This shows how negatively our mind is tuned. Trust is the biggest factor missing here which constantly creates assumptions. So assuming is like dreaming and reality is different, so assuming creates constant negative thoughts. The idea is to keep focusing on our karmas and not to be distracted with the assumptions about the externalities.

We don't trust in the universe or God. God has created rules for running this universe. Until and unless those rules are followed perfectly there will always be negativity and an imbalance created around us.

4.9.18 **CONFIDENT**: If we have self-confidence then we are always filled with positive energy. Lack of confidence is a result of negative thoughts constantly being generated due to many negative qualities. What are the triggers which lead to the lack of confidence leading to unhappiness? When we do not understand destiny, we are not willing to accept unfavourable outcomes due to our expectations. Expectations are out of desires, and desires are out of greed, selfishness, comparison, ego, jealousy, and so on. Therefore, many negative qualities trigger many negative thoughts and it is like a chain reaction with a compounding effect on a person's mind. Therefore, it is very important to understand how a lack of confidence arising out of a lack of understanding of the Dharma, can make one infested with many negative thoughts and ultimately unhappiness. Self Confidence comes from having real knowledge. One should be capable, a good human being, hard-working, loyal, sincere towards others, compassionate, simplicity, etc with good human qualities. Self Confidence comes from following the Dharma close to perfection. Else there will only be the generation of negative thoughts due to a lack of confidence. Pure knowledge and wisdom are the best acquisition to be possessed.

What we need to see is that it is the real inner peace and confidence which gets reflected on our faces and body language. Such people do not have to worry about external decorations to showcase their personalities. What we see in materialistically successful people is Ego and not confidence. Such egoistic people are filled with negativity. They are the leaders of such a corrupt and toxic system that has been created in this world due to their lust and greed. The artificial world we have created into which most of us have been rapidly drifting and have got completely sucked into it. Thereby making it very difficult to come out and realize the reality and live in the reality as per the Dharma. Living in this system is like an addiction. De-addiction is very difficult. Therefore, this book aims to make people realize that you need to get out of this corrupt system else you can never have peace of mind. The advanced or so-called materialistically advanced societies or nations are the ones with maximum mental health issues. High suicide rates, depression, depending on pills, psychologists, etc.

Today's humans are not a reflection of their inside. Outside is all a camouflage of pretence.

4.9.19   **FEARLESS** :   What fear does is well known to us. Fear generates many negative thoughts. What kind of fears do we carry? Fear of losing what we have and fear of not getting what we want. Then there is fear of death. Fear of survival and fear of an uncertain future.

Attachment to this illusionary world is the real cause of fear. Fear of death is due to attachment with this temporary body or identifying ourselves with this mortal body. Desires, greed, and expectations, all create fear. Every expectation triggers the fear of expectations not being met.

Why do such fears come into our minds? Because, we forget about destiny, acceptance, and letting go. These are the main cause. Life is not a constant graph, there are ups and downs. It moves as per our previous karmas. Every karma gets redeemed whenever the time comes for its redemption. This is the holy science. We get what we deserve; we lose what we don't deserve. In other words, we get what we need and we lose what we do not need. There are many ways to look at it. All have subtle differences but deep rooted meanings.

Fear comes from unrealistic desires and expectations, if we have such desires and expectations without realizing whether we can achieve them or not, are we capable of achieving that or not, do we have the potential for that or not, do we have the courage and conviction to carry out the effort to achieve those. Thus, we keep creating castles in the air and unrealistic dreams, comparing ourselves with people around us, leading to the setting of unrealistic targets. This ultimately triggers fear of not getting or achieving it. Fear not only triggers negative thoughts by itself, it also triggers negative thoughts of frustration, anxiety, depression, panic, etc as time passes by. Fear of failure leads to a lack of confidence in oneself and poor decision making abilities.

So it is important to review all the human qualities of selflessness, no greed, and no expectations, and so on to understand how to avoid creation of fearful thoughts.

4.9.20 **GRATITUDE** : Being thankful for someone's help or someone's good gestures or acts. Gratitude is like acknowledging and it sends good vibes to the other person. This in turn builds good bonding and trust. Gratitude can be pegged as a basic courtesy of being thankful and also remembering that someone did something good for you or good to you. Also, gratitude is reciprocating that good gesture when your turn comes to be good to that person. And not being ungrateful.

If we don't have the basic courtesy of gratitude and if we do not reciprocate, then this will eventually leave a bad taste in the relationship and lead to bitterness. Finally triggering a negative thought in your mind, as when you expect the other person to be kind again towards you that person might not be the same again. Then your expectation out of opportunism will fail. So if you don't have gratitude then you are an opportunist. This Karma of opportunism will ultimately catch up with you creating negative thoughts and other issues. Gratitude creates happiness in others and in return you get it back.

4.9.21 **HARDWORKING & RESPONSIBLE**: In human life focus has to be on karma, everything else is a distraction. This is the only recipe for mental peace. Responsibilities are the karmas we need to be performing as we exist in this social system and take the roles as we grow in life. If we do not perform our duties sincerely and perfectly, then the outcomes will not be as per the needs. Thereby, making a negative impact on the people, who will be affected by these outcomes. In turn, making you unhappy with the adverse responses. There is no denying that there are no shortcuts to anything. One has to put best efforts to achieve one's objectives through the tasks. This can further aggravate the relationships, if ego comes in between, and you do not like the adverse responses from others for not fulfilling your duties. Leading to denials and arguments, thus adding more negative thoughts in your mind. Such thoughts, action and reactions make the environment toxic.

Laziness is a big disease in today's society, the younger generation is looking only for short cuts. They are addicted to the digitalized social media. They waste time on useless things. Unethical and corrupted mind, lack of discipline and integrity has become a big social issue pervading today's society. There is too much exposure to too many unwanted things at a young age, as well as even when you are grown up with more responsibilities. Laziness leads to incompetence and subsequently related issues of survival and sustenance. Humans or citizens are pillars of the country and if the generation turns into non productive & irresponsible beings, then that country will finally be doomed, irrespective of what it has been historically. In some countries, people are busy singing their past glories and also blaming others for the present sad state of affairs of that country, while themselves being non productive and irresponsible towards their own objectives.

Outcome of laziness can only be multiple failures. This will only trigger negative thoughts. The word Modern is synonymous with progressive, and ancient with backwardness. In fact, this is a wrong perception created in our mind. It is the modern society which is degrading and it was the ancient system for example ancient Vedic System based on Sanatan dharma which was ideal. Sanatan means immortal and dharma is rule or law. So this was an immortal rule used for the existence and performance of the humans. It is not a religion. It belongs to the humanity and is for the humanity. It is borderless and religion less.

4.9.22 **NOT CONTROLLING** : Why are we trying to control everything and everyone around us? What happens when we try to control, what kind of thoughts will this controlling lead to in your mind? Investigate whether you are a control freak or not. The desire to control mainly comes out of expectations, possessiveness, and ego. When we are unable to control it gives rise to negative thoughts of anger, frustration, hatred, etc. Instead, a supporting approach and a caring approach will help in the situation. Acceptance is needed. We need to focus on our karma and not really on other's karmas. Our ego is a major contributor, which drives us to get into a controlling mode. Everyone needs to be left with their share of responsibilities and let them perform their karma. It is the attachment, ego, and expectations that lead to control. Controlling eventually leads to frustration and anger, and it really does not help either of the affected people.

While managing is different from controlling, so this should not be mixed up with controlling. Managing is needed in any organized society, be it family or any organization, where there are set of rules to be followed and there are review processes to ensure that responsibilities are fulfilled by people. Managing is part of the system or responsibilities. Trying to force control people beyond a point is what we are discussing here. Beyond a critical mass limit, if we try to control, then it may not be beneficial and may not yield the desired results of making the other person perform. Each individual has its strong habits and is groomed in a way that it becomes typical of his/her characteristics. Everyone needs to evolve and that is why this book is an effort for people to use it for evolving as a better human being.

One has to accept after a point and focus on own tasks, as it is ultimately the destiny and we cannot change or transform anyone else. Trying to control will only lead us to losing our peace of mind.

4.9.23 **SIMPLICITY** : Simplicity provides peace of mind as one focuses on basic needs and does not go behind the glamour and show-biz. When we flow with the consumerism, materialistic success and fake identities, for so called fake acceptance and acknowledgment in this artificial society, then we move far away from a simple living. That is when we lose our peace of mind, as we are in a wild goose chase, chasing an illusion and living a hell of a life with no peace of mind. Happiness and success from this glitz and glamour is itself an illusion and one can never get that happiness, instead, it is only the ego that goes up. We only end up being a snob, and slowly we create distances from our near and dear ones. We associate ourselves with the artificial people who are there till the time you have your identity, once your identity changes all of them vanish in the thin air. One can have long discussions on this. In short, do think about what simplicity is and how it provides you happiness. It is logical that as you make your life more complex, it is bound to create a lifestyle imbalance. The opposite of SIMPLICITY is COMPLEXITY.

4.9.24 **AUSTERITY** : Tell me, is a rich man more happy or a yogi in the Himalayas is more happy? Is happiness defined by money and fake identities? Do people with less materialistic possessions are having more fake people, and more true relations around them compared to rich people? Are people relating to you because of your intrinsic human qualities or based on your materialistic status?

What is austerity? It is about relinquishing materialistic comforts and being close to nature. We need to deeply understand that, what are the basic needs and what are desires. This will sound very radical to most of us as we are deeply entrenched in this materialistic way of living. Though many are realizing the benefit of simplicity and austerity and moving to the rural lifestyle. Austerity makes one close to the nature and with completely reduced dependency on the capitalistic and consumerist society. You become self-reliant. Life otherwise, has become very complex, and this adds to many unwanted complications and added burdens, just in order to maintain and manage the assets. This leads to constant worries or negative thoughts. Depriving one, their peace of mind. Austerity helps in getting liberated from one's ego and artificial identity. Here we are completely inert to the externalities, and completely detached from the illusionary world. The whole point of discussion here is peace of mind or meditative state of mind, with consistency.

4.9.25   **LOVE** : Some of the qualities like love are not the core qualities. Love is a sum total of all the good human qualities. All other qualities when present in pure & positive form create an act or thought of love. The Karma based on love is actually the true Dharma. This is what true love is. What we think about true love between two people is actually just an impulsive attraction with a desire of acquiring and possessing that person and later metamorphosing that into a relationship built on control, expectations, and fulfillment of selfish desires. True love has to be unconditional, that means if all the human qualities are fully on the positive side then the love naturally becomes unconditional. Conditions are nothing but based on ego and other negative human qualities. Conditions based on negative qualities make the love impure. The mind is purified when every thought and action is filled with true love. It is also needed to introspect, why one should love someone more, and someone less. In humanity, this whole world is one family. There is true equality created by the creator in this universe. When you realize that all are equal then where is the question of loving someone more than other. This again leads to conditioning while dealing with different people. There is a difference between loving your family more and others less. It is actually like having a family as a direct responsibility, and that does not mean that you love your family more. This is actually an attachment we create towards our family and that is not really love.

Imagine if every interaction between every two-person was always filled with unconditional true love, then how much love and harmony will be there in this world. What we see as love is actually an attraction, attachment, and lust. All negative qualities finally lead to suffering. True love is eternal and permanent, what we perceive as love, is a transient thought, that changes with the constantly changing human behaviour.

So if there is always true love in every thought and action, then the mind will always be in a state of bliss. No negative thoughts. That is the purification of mind and true liberation of humans from all the worldly miseries.

4.9.26 **ANGER** : Again like Love, Anger is also not the core human quality but it is an outcome of a few of the core qualities which are tuned negatively in a person. Anger can lead to stress, anxiety, depression, diseases, etc. It affects health in many ways.

When we have unwanted desires, they give rise to expectations, intolerance, impatience, and subsequently anger. So if we get angry often, then it is required to check other negative qualities, which need to be reined in and removed. So that anger is not generated.

Anger is sometimes required in a way, that one should show anger without getting angry. There is a difference between getting angry and showing anger. Showing anger is like showing firmness while managing work from other people and ensuring discipline, etc.

4.9.27 **HEALTH** : Good health is important for a healthy mind. If our health is not good then this problem will trigger many negative qualities like fear, anxiety, inability to perform certain tasks, lack of confidence, etc. Thereby, giving rise to many negative thoughts. In fact, negative thoughts ultimately act on the body itself and cause health issues. Diseases are not caused by external factors directly, but through the mind. Do a deep dive to understand this. Also if one needs to sit in an asan (posture), then one has to master that posture. For the duration one has to meditate, say for an hour, the body is required to remain absolutely still without causing any discomfort. Otherwise, the body itself will become a source of disturbance and distraction in the practice of meditation. Many people come to a meditation class and think that the teacher will do some magic and they will have some magical experience of meditation, without even understanding that, if they cannot even sit properly and still for some time, then how will they be able to focus in meditation. None of the meditation teachers will tell this to their students, as in the beginning itself it will become a non-starter for their business.

4.9.28 **ACCEPTANCE** : What happens when we do not accept unfavourable situations, or anything not meeting our expectations, or some desire not getting fulfilled, or when we lose something, or if there is some loss. It makes us unhappy. Now what is destiny? So if we remember destiny, then we will take such unfavourable situations differently and start accepting them. Thereby, become inert to all the so called worldly unfavourable situations. If we don't accept the outcomes and the happenings in our lives, then we will remain unhappy forever, filled with thoughts of non acceptance and many more negative thoughts.

4.9.29 **SURRENDER** : Once we have realized that acceptance is a must, and destiny is also understood well. Also when we realize that it is only karma that needs to be focused on, with pure love as the ingredient of Karma. That's when we are ready to surrender to the creator. It is our ego that makes us feel, that we are the ones who is making things happen. If that was true, then can you give assurance that whatever you want in life, you will be able to make it happen? The only thing we can do in this world in our life is selfless Karma based on Dharma. Based on every action, redemptions happen, whenever they have to happen, at the time scheduled, in the queue of redemption of Karma. Therefore, it is wise to surrender in a way, to the creator. What it means is, that we stop thinking that we are the one who is making it happen. This egoistic thought needs to be dissolved, else, there is a possibility of failing, and then triggering many negative thoughts. We can have intentions to achieve our goals, and make sincere efforts, being truthful to ourselves and others involved with that act. Self-effort is the only way out, if you are really serious about self-transformation. The books or anyone else can only be a guide to you to some extent. After a time, one has to explore oneself.

** *"BY NOW I HAVE TOUCHED UPON ALMOST 30 HUMAN QUALITIES AND I CAN GO ON BUT THEN IT WILL AMOUNT TO SPOON FEEDING AND THE WHOLE SUBJECT WILL BECOME VERY BORING INCLUDING READING THIS SECTION OF DHARMA IN THIS BOOK. THEREFORE, I WOULD STOP HERE AND LEAVE IT FOR YOU TO DO INTROSPECTION ABOUT ALL THE POSSIBLE HUMAN QUALITIES YOURSELF"*

CHAPTER – 5

ENERGY FIELD AND MIND

5.1   When we observe and understand that the thoughts that flow through the nerves are actually an electric signal. We all know that electric signals are actually carrying energy. The whole universe is nothing but a constant flow of energy that keeps changing form. Therefore, when we study how a thought is created in the mind by studying the origin of thought, and thought being an output of some input, then we will understand that it has to have a component of energy. Thought is an output of inputs from the sensory organs. The output will act on the body. The energy created by this output will get transformed and will have an impact on the functioning of the human body.

5.2   Whenever we act our soul is always trying to guide us and tell us what needs to be done as per the human design, but most of us ignore the call of the soul and follow our mind which is working based on our present operating characteristics of the human design. The soul is embedded with the true qualities of the human being and the soul is the purest form of consciousness. The soul is immortal too. Consciousness is the ever pervading omnipresent energy

5.3 We are living in a constantly changing energy field which has its effect not only on us but on living beings around us as well. I am sure we all understand the energy field and its effect. Based on the energy field, we are many times able to say that, so and so person is very negative, or so and so person is very positive. We call it intuition or gut feeling, but we never analyzed what is that gut feeling, or what is that which we call intuition. What flows between two people even if not very close physically, but still intuition tells something about the person we come across. We also say body language, so what is body language. What is exchanged through body language? Women so often can judge which man they can trust. What tells them so? We have never tried to analyze all this.

5.4   The energy created by the thoughts in the mind has its consolidated electromagnetic field. As the thought is created by processing input signals coming to the brain from the sensory organs or the memory. The nerves are the carriers of energy, carrying the encoded signal. Technically our body is just like any other machine. Every creation in this universe has to be scientific, and science is based on logic. The creation itself is a vast science.

This field created by the energy of thoughts is also known as Aura. When we come across a self-realized person, then the feeling is very different in the presence of that person. Only thing is that, we don't try to understand that scientifically, or we do not realize the science behind it.

5.5 When a person is highly positively charged, the energy of such a person will be resonating with the energy of the universe. Basically, that person gets aligned to the universal law. In such a situation, the person appears to be manifesting a lot of his/her thoughts, due to being in resonance with the universal consciousness. Many experiences happen as mind purification progresses due to this resonance or alignment. People start to guess and claim some supernatural developments in them. When we reach such a stage in our practice, and when there is resonance with the universe, then our mind starts giving us experiences which are not limited to the dimensions of space and time. The mind is very powerful and its power is tapped, as we progress towards self-realization.

5.6   You all must have experienced sometimes that whenever we remember someone far off, that person initiates some form of communication. We call it telepathy. This is connected consciousness and nothing else. This is through our energy field, which is part of the collective energy field. The tinkering we are doing through technology misuse or abuse is also leading to harmful effects on our health. Though, these are not tangible, so remain debatable, but if you agree that any input to the existing energy field will make an impact, then we should try to understand how their impact will be on the individual energy fields.

CHAPTER – 6

AFFECT OF MIND ON HEALTH

6.1   Who controls the functioning of all the organs and the systems inside our body ? It has to be none other than the mind or the brain to be more precise. All the internal functions are happening automatically, as they are pre-programmed in the brain. The body not only performs its internal routine functions, but also has a mechanism to fight diseases and heal itself. Therefore, it has been scientifically designed to operate correctly, until and unless external factors influence it, causing internal malfunction or imbalance.

6.2   The whole body is functioning scientifically as well as logically. For such a complex system to function, it has to have a master which is actually the brain. The brain works like the CPU – Central Processing Unit, of the human body. It is sending all the necessary commands to all the organs and the systems for their effective and optimal functioning.

6.3   Therefore, any unwanted input to the brain which is not needed for the proper functioning of the body, will cause an adverse affect on the functioning of the body. We need to note that, the external unwanted influences to the brain are logical (not physical) in nature. They are nothing but the negative or unwanted thoughts. When we say that we are mentally exhausted or feeling stressed, then that is basically the affect of negative thought generation which is causing the mind to overwork and in turn the brain is producing the negative thoughts which is creating a negative field which then acts on the body itself. As a result there is an unnecessary energy required to balance this affect of negative force created by the brain which is acting on the body. The body in turn has to use internal resources and energy to neutralize this detrimental energy. This makes us feel stressed. When this happens at a regular interval with more consistency and increasing intensity, it leads to some imbalance in the internal organs and the systems in our body, thereby, causing illness.

6.4 Human body gets three kinds of inputs; one is through the mind which is the signals from the sensory organs or the memory. Second is food and oxygen, which are needed for providing the necessary energy to the body. Third is external force through exercise for the physical endurance and fitness of the muscles. So apart from the mind, we need to ensure that we understand these needs of the body as well and be conscious about our eating habits and lifestyle. Simple and healthy eating is what is needed. The science of Ayurveda deals with these basics of nutrition and internal physical well being. Yoga asanas is the science of fitness and strength. Meditation is the science of mind purification and mind control. Together, these are required to ensure a complete and comprehensive healthy living, mentally as well as physically. This in totality is a yogic science as well as the "Law of Nature" or the "Law of Karma and Dharma".

View from Almora, Himalayas - India

CHAPTER – 7

SPIRITUALITY - CONCEPTS

7.1 Spirituality is nothing but humanity. Spirituality is basically doing karma as per Dharma. This is a very short definition of spirituality. The quest for the truth about human being's existence and operation is a quest for spirit and soul. Being in the process of this discovery is spirituality. When one starts seeking and exploring correctly then only one progresses spiritually otherwise rest all are egoistic assumptions to make one feel good and superior.

7.2 When something unknown happens within their body or in the mind, people start telling that they have become spiritual. People who are visiting temples, etc also claim to be spiritual. Even a criminal goes to a temple, which does not mean he/she has turned spiritual. In reality, if you are chasing and executing wrong thoughts through bad karma, then one cannot claim to be spiritual.

7.3   Spirituality is not a self-acclaimed stamp to self-certify oneself. Spiritual path is very personal, and anything in that path is not be used for proving oneself as a good human being.

7.4   When one is really on the right path, one will gradually build relationships with spiritual people, and start distancing themselves with the worldly people.

7.5   Escapism from worldly responsibilities or karma is not spirituality. That is actually being lazy.

7.6   In spirituality one has to be just aware about their Karmas and following the Dharma.

7.7   Our destiny is created by our own actions. Every action has to have an outcome. Every input has to create an output. This is the law of transformation   or   conversion   of   energy. Thoughts lead to actions which are karma.   If Karma is based on Dharma (good qualities) then the outcomes will be good, thereby, creating a favourable destiny for us or a good future for us. There is also a saying, "As you sow, so shall you reap". These sayings are like the wise quotes, very well time tested since ages. Actually, the life experience's teach us, and make us understand all this as there are many proofs in our own life which can lead to the correct interpretations and conclusions. This is what is introspective, and experiential learning through the book called life.

7.8 Manifestations happen when we are aligned to the dharma, in other words, we are in resonance with the cosmic flow of the energy without being an obstacle to that flow. Our mind becomes or creates those obstacles, when we are not basing our actions as per the dharma or the law of the nature. Manifestations are nothing but all good outcomes which will happen from good karmas. One cannot manifest unwanted desires as that itself will lead to wrong expectations and going out of alignment with the flow of cosmic energy.

7.9 Spiritual experiences are nothing but the experience of bliss arising out of purification of the mind and the body. This can lead to many experiences which cannot be experienced in the present dimensions of time and space. Such experiences can give us strong intuition, visions and clarity. They also make us realize that this world is an illusion and there is some mystical power which is beyond this illusion. Even if you meet a self realized person who is fully connected to his soul, you can feel the bliss just by being in his/her presence.

7.10 Some Spiritual Bullets

7.10.1   "Don't try to make it happen, instead, allow it to happen"

7.10.2   "The world is an Illusion or rather, whatever is visible is an illusion"

7.10.3   "The whole world is a family and all are equal" – Oneness.

7.10.4   "Every object in this world, be it a stone, has life, as it has a material composition, therefore, it has energy. Energy is life"

7.10.5   "Try to feel the vibrations of the place or a person"

7.10.6   "Face and Body reflects the energy field of a person and it tells what state of mind they possess"

7.10.7   "Guru will emerge when you have made sincere effort to progress on your spiritual path" The Guru is inside you only. Life around us is also a Guru, as it teaches us. We learn from everything we see or come across, provided we are open to learning and receiving.

7.10.8   "Love all and Serve all"

7.10.9   "Happiness is omnipresent; it is not to be sought. Happiness is not bound by time and space. So there is no need to go anywhere. We only have to remove the veil of ignorance and illusion to uncover that ever present happiness inside us".

7.10.10   **"Opposite of MEDITATION is DISTRACTION"** – so identify your distractions and the cause of distractions and then work to eliminate the causes of distractions. *Mind you, the causes are your own negative qualities, and not the object which you feel is distracting you.*

7.10.11 "Do not pretend to meditate" "Do not get fooled by the businessmen running meditation courses"

7.10.12 "Simplicity, Austerity, and renunciation are the indications of a real yogi or saint" others are worldly ones pretending to be a real one. Real yogis will be far away from fame, glitz, glamour and money.

7.10.13 "Don't announce that you are a spiritual person, as that is only your ego making you feel good or justify your present situation. Be truthful to yourself, else your life will flow like that of an ignorant lazy person"

7.10.14 "Complete detachment is very difficult to achieve. Then only one can reach total liberation of our mind from this illusionary world". Making our mind totally at peace and bliss. Constant effort is required".

7.10.15   "Joy of Giving is the best joy to be experienced" Not everyone is fortunate to experience joy of giving. Not everyone gets the opportunity to experience the joy of giving." Without generosity one cannot have this. Serving selflessly is the only karma we undertake, and that can only give us the joy of giving.

7.10.16   "Karma & Dharma" is the only secret to happiness, and liberation from the slavery of our mind. Karma and Dharma is nothing else, but the law of the nature or the law made by the creator.

7.10.17   "What do you call that being who created this universe and is managing it" ?

7.10.18   "Imagine you don't have a name, how will you describe yourself and compare yourself with another person".

7.10.19   "If you are belonging to a particular religion, have you read the religious book yourself and understood it"? Then what is your opinion about your religion? Should you give your opinion about a religion without reading and understanding it

7.10.20   "If you stop comparing yourself with others, do you feel you will be able to experience oneness with this universe"?

CHAPTER – 8

MYTHS ABOUT MEDITATION

8.1 No worldly teacher has any magic technique or any magical powers which can take you to the meditative state while they make you sit with your eyes closed.

8.2 Guided meditation is just a term coined to misguide people, as no teacher can guide you into a meditative state. Those looking only for guided meditation are the ones who don't want to make their own efforts.

8.3 Meditation is actually a state to be attained through constant transformation one has to bring in due course of time with a constant practice of introspection. The word used to describe the practice in Indian language is SADHANA.

8.4 Sitting with closed eyes cannot remove worries from your mind, intermittent removal does happen when we create another distraction like teachers tell you to focus on breath. So for some time, one is able to focus on breath and able to get rid of distractions. After this sitting, the mind is back to the same state of chaos. So this is just a trick to make you attempt meditation by the unrealized teachers or inexperienced teachers, who lack self-awareness. Meditation is not about having a momentary pleasant feeling, for the duration of the class.

8.5   Also, even if anywhere a teacher makes you sit, and you think you will do some meditation, then first of all you should be able to sit still in the suggested posture, which itself is not possible for most people. So practice is needed even to sit still for longer time. Idea is to reach a state of calm in mind consistently and not just when you sit.

8.6   Mind is like an engine which is constantly running and when we try to meditate in some guided meditation or some technique, we are able to switch off this engine or slow it down. So this experience gives some calmness and we feel we achieved something in meditation. Therefore, without knowing the definition and purpose and process of meditation, it is a waste of time and energy. When the mind is being constantly thinking it is being constantly utilized which means the engine is constantly running, which means that we are constantly dissipating energy in useless things or thoughts. Mind should be parked like a car when not in use, and only started when needed and used effectively with full focus.

REFERENCES AND INSPIRATIONS

9.1　My **YouTube Channel** by name "**Shiv Mathur**" – it has videos in five categories.

9.1.1 Yogis I found in the Himalayas who seem to be self realized

9.1.2 Meditation philosophy

9.1.3 Spirituality

9.1.4 Spiritual Travel

9.1.5 Devotional Chants, Bhajans & Kirtans from off-beat places

9.2　Devotional music from various artists

9.3　Inspired by the teachings and pull of the following yogis and saints :

9.3.1　Swami Vivekananda

9.3.2　Maa Anandamayee

9.3.3　Ramana Maharishi

9.3.4　Paramhansa Yogananda

9.3.5 Swami Rama

9.3.6 Neemkaroli Baba

9.3.7 Nisargdutta Guru Maharaj

9.3.8   Tatwale Baba ji

9.3.9   Acharya Bhaskar Joshi ji

9.3.10 Shri Yukteshwar Giri ji maharaj

For any feedback or clarification or any other need I am sharing my mail id below and the YouTube channel link :-

My e-mail id :

shivmathur0903@gmail.com

You Tube channel :

http://youtube.com/c/ShivMathur

TATWALE
BABA

MAA
ANANDAMAYEE

RAMANA
MAHARISHI

NEEMKAROLI
BABA

NISARGDUTTA GURU JI MAHARAJ

SWAMI RAMA

SHRI YUKTESHWAR GIRI JI MAHARAJ

PARAMHANSA YOGANANDA

SWAMI VIVEKANANDA

ACHARYA BHASKAR JOSHI JI

<u>My likely Next book</u>

Title   :   "Spiritual Encounters"

Sub-title :   Meeting the Himalayan Yogis

Reference :   YouTube video on my channel
                         "My Spiritual Journey Part-1
                         and Part-2" are a short
                         summary of what will come in
                         the book in detail.